Guinea Pigs

How to care for your Guinea Pig and everything you need to know to keep them well

BY

DR. GORDON ROBERTS BVSC MRCVS

Table of Contents

INTRODUCTION

PART 1: THE GUINEA PIG REVEALED
WHAT'S IN A NAME?
ORIGINS AND HISTORY
PHYSICAL CHARACTERISTICS
SENSORY ABILITIES
BEHAVIOUR
DIET IN THE WILD
BREEDING
CHILDREN AND GUINEA PIGS

PART 2: CHOOSING A GUINEA PIG
GENDER
AGE
HEALTH
PERSONALITY
ONE, TWO, OR MORE?
WHERE TO FIND?

PART 3: CARING FOR YOUR GUINEA PIG
HOUSING
OUTDOOR HOUSING
BEDDING
FEEDING AND NUTRITION
GROOMING AND BATHING
CLEANLINESS
HEALTH AND ILLNESS
FINDING A VETERINARIAN

PART 4: GUINEA PIGS AT WORK AND PLAY
COMMUNICATION
TRAINING—TECHNIQUES
TRAINING—THINGS TO TRAIN
TOYS
ENVIRONMENT
ADDING PLAYMATES
CONCLUSION
APPENDIX 1: NAMING YOUR PET

Introduction

Guinea pigs have been a popular pet since at least the late 16th century. So: why guinea pigs? Since you're reading this book, you'll be pleased to know that there are MANY reasons!

Here they are. Guinea pigs are fantastic pets because:
- They are gentle;
- They are good natured;
- They don't need long walks;
- They are compact and don't need a lot of room;
- They are easy to care for;
- They can be trained;
- They are fun and funny to be around;
- They are cheap to keep and feed;
- They are fine pets whether you live in the city or the country;
- They can be kept inside or outside;
- They come in a variety of different coats and colours,
- But most of all…because they're irresistibly cute!

Guinea pigs are amazing pets for children but, in fact they're really great for people of all ages. With the tips and information in this book, you'll be able to keep your guinea pig(s) healthy, happy and comfortable, and in return your guinea pig(s) will make YOU happy! (Any effect on your health and comfort is just a bonus!)

Part 1:
The Guinea Pig Revealed

The guinea pig feels like a pretty familiar animal to most of us, and the reasons are not hard to find, after. all, they're commonly found in zoos and are a popular pet. , One 2007 survey estimated a population of 1.35 million of guinea pigs in the USA. That's not exactly cat or dog numbers (88.3 million and 74.8 million respectively, for the curious), but it's certainly enough that the majority of people have come into contact with guinea pigs by the time they reach adulthood.

For all that familiarity though, how much do you really know about guinea pigs? There's a lot more to the guinea pig story than you might think, and in this Part of the book we pull back the curtain and reveal some of the essential facts that you will need to know as a guinea pig owner.

You know how 'guinea pig' is an epithet for a test subject? During the 19th and 20th centuries, the cavies were regularly used a 'model organisms' in testing - just another way that guinea pigs have given something back to their human masters!

Physical Characteristics

Cavies are rodents—meaning that they are mammals of the order Rodentia, like beavers, hamsters, and rats—and they share common physical characteristics with other rodents. For example, they have incisor teeth that grow continuously, and must be worn down by gnawing. The process of wearing down the incisors by gnawing keeps the incisors razor sharp, and this is reckoned to be a key characteristic that helps rodents survive and thrive (and hey, it beats brushing!). Also, like many rodents, guinea pigs are small: typically from 700 to 1200 g (1.5–2.5 pounds) in weight, and 20 to 25 cm (8–10 inches) in length. This is actually large compared with rodents in general, though they seem small to us.

What else? Guinea pigs don't have tails, do have whiskers, have three toes on each hind paw but four on each front paw, have short legs, and are 'stout' in the best possible way!

Sensory Abilities

Like most rodents, guinea pigs have highly advanced senses of smell and touch. Their sight is reckoned to be not as good as a typical human's, though the location of their eyes on either side of their heads gives them better peripheral vision than ours. The hairs (whiskers) on their muzzles, known as vibrissae, are used to measure openings. Like cats, cavies use these hairs to determine accurately whether their bodies will be able to fit through an opening when the light is poor or non-existent (for example, in a burrow).

Guinea pigs also have sensitive hearing, which of course they need in the wild to help them detect stealthy predators. In captivity, you might find that your cavy's hearing is so acute that it gets excited when you open the fridge door or rustle a bag—noises it might associate with food. Keep in mind that guinea pigs startle easily at loud noises, so be aware and try to keep those to a minimum.

Behaviour

In the wild, the ancestors of guinea pigs would have had a lot of predators, and in order to avoid being eaten, would have been constantly on the lookout for danger. Modern guinea pigs haven't lost this trait, and so you will notice that your pet can appear to you to be nervy and highly strung. (Another way to put this is to say that guinea pigs are highly alert, which is very common behaviour for prey animals in the wild.)

To avoid giving your guinea pig any unnecessary stress, it's important that you try not to act like a predator. What does this mean? Well, it means not grabbing your cavy from above, as this is how a bird of prey would attack. Instead, talk to your cavy softly and kindly for at least a few seconds before touching him or her. It also means keeping your guinea pig in a quiet part of your house, refraining from any fast or aggressive movements, and not disturbing him or her when they are sleeping.

Another behavioural trait that the ancestors of guinea pigs had was that of being crepuscular, which means that they were most active at twilight—that is, at dawn and dusk. This behaviour is thought to be an 'anti-predator' adaptation, as most predators are either night or day hunters. In captivity, cavies mostly lose this trait and conform to human patterns.

Diet in the Wild

In the wild guinea pigs eat mostly grass, and actually need to eat grass or hay to maintain proper digestive health. They crop the grass with their incisors and then grind it with their molars, which are highly suited to this task.

Grass is of course difficult to digest; there's a reason cows have four stomachs! Guinea pigs get around this problem through the practice of 'coprophagy'. This means that, like rabbits, they eat their own faeces after it has been through them once. This gives their digestive tracts a second chance to extract nutrients from the grass that they ate.

Breeding

You're might be thinking that anything related to rats and mice probably breeds often, quickly, and in large numbers. This educated guess is entirely correct! Guinea pigs breed year-round, pregnancy lasts only about 65 days on average, and while litters average three pups, up to six is not uncommon.

Unlike most other rodents, guinea pigs give birth to young that are 'precocial', which means 'relatively mature and mobile from the moment of birth'. They are born with teeth, are able to eat solid food straightaway, and will reach sexual maturity themselves just 3-5 weeks later.

Children and Guinea Pigs

Do you have children? If you're reading this book, it's a fair bet that you do. Perhaps your main motivation for getting a cavy is so that your children will have a pet. Pets and children of course go hand-in-hand, and guinea pigs and children even more so!

First off, let's make one thing clear: guinea pigs are a wonderful pet for children. They are gentle, just the right size, interesting, fun in general, fun to feed, attention-loving, cute, and they make adorable little squeals and grunts. So far, so good.

Now for the bad news. Families with children are far, far more likely to dump, abandon or give guinea pigs up for adoption than adults-only families. Why? Because even the most diligent and animal-loving child can, and probably will, get bored of a guinea pig pet long before the guinea pig lives out a normal span of years. Children are more or less famous for losing interest in pets once the novelty has worn off. Unfortunately, the lesson here is that you really shouldn't get a guinea pig for your children unless you are ok with doing all (and we do mean all) of the work yourself.

Also, don't kid yourself that you will be able to teach your child responsibility that he or she currently lacks through feeding and cleaning chores. Showing children that good things in life (like a lovely pet to cuddle) don't come without hard work (like cleaning out a dirty cage once a week) sounds plausible in principle, but at the end of the day it's just not fair for an animal in your care to have to rely, even in part, on the whims of a child.

With those warnings out of the way, we can consider some other issues relating to children and cavies, and chief among these is safety. Guinea pigs are small and therefore easily hurt, even by children and even by accident.

Toddler-age children simply won't have the awareness that is required to keep a guinea pig safe. In fact, as a rule of thumb, children aged 5 and under should be supervised at all times when handling cavies. Have them sit on the floor before they are allowed to handle the guinea pig(s), don't let them walk around carrying a guinea pig, and don't allow your pets to have free floor time until your children are tucked up in bed.

Beyond this, the other important rule to follow is that an adult should always be responsible for overseeing a pet's health and well-being. Your children might be responsible for feeding, watering and cleaning, but you should be checking regularly to ensure that your guinea pig is healthy and happy. A word of caution in relation to visitors. It's only natural that when your children have friends over they will want to show off their pet. Even if the other children are well-intentioned and seem responsible, you simply can't trust other children to know how to treat an unfamiliar pet, and as we have previously noted, cavies are small and easily injured. For these reasons you should ensure that there is constant adult supervision whenever children are visiting, until you are 100% that the other children know the correct way of handling and treating your pet.

Finally, if you have children and want them to get excited about guinea pigs before their new pet arrives, below are two great children's books about guinea pigs to whet their appetites.

John Willy & Freddy McGee, written and illustrated by Holly Meade. This is a story about two extraordinary guinea pigs that start out in ordinary (and therefore rather boring) circumstances. When the chance comes for them to escape their cage, they seize it with both paws! This book really emphasises the charming and playful nature of guinea pigs. It's a great adventure story and a fun book to read aloud. For ages 3-5.

Olga Carries On, written by Michael Bond and illustrated by Hans Helweg. You might recognise the name Michael Bond OBE, as he's the best-selling author of the Paddington Bear series of books. This title is one of the 'Olga da Polga' series that all feature the same adventurous, imaginative and unstoppable female guinea pig. Olga lives with the Sawdust family and is primarily cared for by young Karen Sawdust. In this instalment of Olga's outings, Olga meets some new arrivals in the Sawdust family and treats them to a poetry recital! This is 160 pages and for ages 8 and up.

Part 2: Choosing a Guinea Pig

It would be nice if, having decided to get a pet, the perfect one (or two) just knocked on the door! But unfortunately, you have to search out and buy pets just like you do everything else. So what's the best way of going about this in the case of guinea pigs? Read on to find out about this and much more.

Gender

There is considerable debate about whether male or female guinea pigs make better pets. Really, it depends on you and what you're looking for in a pet. Broadly speaking, boars (males) tend to be bolder, cheekier, and more robust. Sows (females) on the other hand tend to be calmer and gentler, and like to snuggle more. Having said this, individual personality counts for a lot, and so you will find bold sows and calm boars.

While we're on the subject of gender, how do you tell a male guinea pig from a female? First of all by their size, as males are usually larger than females. Beyond that it's a matter of flipping them over and checking their genitals. Pressing gently on a boar's belly will cause his penis to emerge (technically, it will, 'extrude'). Sows on the other hand have a smooth swelling over their genital area. If you gently part the genital opening on a sow you should see a 'Y'.

Note that it's common for people to think that having a guinea pig spayed or neutered will alter its personality. This is partly true, depending on your definition of personality! De-sexing (that is, spraying or neutering) will not affect your cavy's personality except to reduce sexual and hormone-related behaviours.

Where gender really does become an issue is when you have more than one guinea pig. For more on this, see further on.

Age

Guinea pigs must be at least four weeks old before they are separated from their mothers. They need this initial period to grow up normally and in good health. Beyond this, it doesn't really matter how old or young the guinea pig you choose is…though of course, the older he or she is, the less time you will get to spend together.

The only real caveat is that guinea pigs need to be handled from a young age in order to be comfortable with it. If you're buying from a breeder (see below) that is unlikely to be an issue, but if not—and if you are considering a more mature cavy—then investigate whether your prospective pet is comfortable with being handled before you commit.

Health

It's pretty unlikely that anyone will try to sell you a sick guinea pig. Having said that, it doesn't hurt to know a few basic things to watch out for, particularly if you aren't buying from a breeder (more on this later on).

Here's a short checklist:
- Ears and nose—are they clean, with no discharge? Any lice in the ears?
- Fur—should be glossy and soft with no bare patches.
- Abdomen—if it is unusually hard and round, your prospective pet may have worms.
- Teeth—should be correctly aligned, meaning that the upper incisors overlap the lower incisors.
- General demeanour—here you're looking for an animal that is bright eyed and alert. As for people, a dull or listless attitude is usually a sign of ill health.

Personality

Guinea pigs, of course, have different personalities, just like every other animal. For example, some are mellow, while some are high-strung. And that's a good thing, because it would be pretty boring if they all behaved in identical ways. Part of the fun of being a pet owner is taking pleasure in what your pet does differently from other animals you've known of the same species.

Let's say you want a cavy with a particular type of personality though. How do you go about assessing a guinea pig's personality quickly enough for it to inform your decision of which one to get? The short answer is that you can't, not really—learning about a pet's personality is a journey of discovery that takes weeks and months.

Having said that, there are a few things you can do. First of all, take as much time as you can getting to know your prospective pet before you commit to keeping it. Second, if you are buying from a breeder, talk to them. They are generally experts in cavy behaviour and should be able to give you a good rundown of what they know about the personalities of the guinea pigs in their care. And lastly, get your prospective pet out of its cage and see how it reacts to you, and you to it. You can tell a lot just by cuddling!

One, Two, or More?

As we'll discuss later, guinea pigs are gregarious creatures. In the wild, they live in groups of ten or more, so living alone is pretty unnatural for them. That's not to say that keeping just one is wrong, but it is true that guinea pigs benefit greatly from having company. On the other hand, when you're deciding how many guinea pigs to acquire, there are a few things to consider mind.

First, there is space to consider. A cage with internal dimensions of about 1m x 0.5m x 0.25m high (see Part 3, below) is big enough for one cavy. Beyond that, you can follow a rule of about a 60cm x 60cm cube (0.25m high) per animal. This means that you don't need a significantly bigger cage for two cavies, but for 3+ the space requirements increase pretty quickly.

Second, you should think about time. A second cavy certainly won't double the amount of time you need to spend caring for your rodent pets, but it will increase it somewhat (say about 25%). If you are already stretched caring for one cavy, maybe a second isn't a good idea.

Finally, you want to consider how your pets will interact with each other. Two or more females are fine together, whether de-sexed or not. Two or more males, on the other hand, will fight unless they are neutered. And if you mix genders, you will of course need to have them all spayed/neutered. If you don't, you will quickly have a lot more guinea pigs than you ever intended to!

Where to Find?

As is the case for most pets, the best way to buy a guinea pig is from a responsible breeder. Good breeders are passionate about their animals, keep their charges clean and healthy, are experts who can give you helpful advice, and keep track of bloodlines so that you can find out about your pet's lineage.

How do you know a good breeder from a not-so-good one? Here is a brief list of 'tells':

- A good breeder will welcome you in and let you see every part of their breeding operation, so that you can determine for yourself the conditions that their cavies are raised in. A bad breeder will seek to hide the rough edges of their operation from you so that you don't see unclean conditions or less-than-healthy animals.
- A good breeder will be passionate about cavies, and eager to share their knowledge with new people. A bad breeder will lack this enthusiasm.
- A good breeder will be full of helpful advice and will want to teach you how to properly care for your new pet—a bad breeder won't care.
- Finally, a good breeder will likely be involved in 'the cavy fancy' (i.e. showing guinea pigs in competitions) in some way. A bad breeder will only be in it for the money, and so will see this side of things as a waste of time.

Guinea pigs are discarded and made homeless just like cats and dogs, and for this reason it's also worth considering adoption. It can be a little bit hard to find a guinea pig in need of adoption, but start by contacting animal shelters in your area. Note that if you visit an animal shelter in person, you might need to ask whether they have any cavies, as they might be kept away from the cats and dogs behind closed doors.

If you don't have any luck with animal shelters in your area, your next best bet is to ask at local vet surgeries. Failing that, try some internet searches. There might be an animal rescue association or similar that will be very happy to hear from you.

Of course, adopting a guinea pig is a whole different kettle of fish to buying one from a respected breeder. An adopted pet might be of uncertain background, with undiagnosed health problems, personality issues and so forth. Have a good think about whether you are willing and able to deal with these sorts of unknowns before you adopt!

But what about the elephant in the room, pet shops? We've left pet shops until last because honestly, it's hard to recommend them. Most of them don't look after their animals properly, and while there are definitely exceptions, the good ones are unfortunately in the minority. It's quite common to see guinea pigs in pet shops being kept in dirty cages, sharing with rabbits, with inadequate hay, no nest boxes, inappropriate food, and no fresh water available. All of these are warning signs that you should shop elsewhere.

If you see guinea pigs being kept in substandard conditions in a pet shop it's tempting to rescue one by buying it, but this really just perpetuates a cycle. Far better if the conditions are really bad to report the pet shop to the authorities, who will hopefully compel them to rectify things or shut down.

Part 3:
Caring for your Guinea Pig

Every child gets a lecture about this from their parents, but even so, it's worth repeating the following: deciding to get any pet entails taking on a big responsibility. A little creature will be utterly dependant on you for food, water, shelter, medical care, and so on, and for a period of probably at least five years. In Part 3, we will consider every meaningful aspect of keeping a guinea pig happy and healthy.

Housing

Like most rodent pets, guinea pigs need a cage to keep them safe and warm when you aren't holding or playing with them. The minimum size for one cavy is probably bigger than you'd expect, at 1m x 0.5m x 0.25m high. This allows room to move around and stretch out, while also accommodating a nest box, food and water, and some toys. It also allows your guinea pig to 'stand' on his hind legs without his head touching the top of the cage.

If you can afford and have room in your house for a larger cage, definitely get one; bigger is better when it comes to housing your little furry pal. When you start to shop for a cage, you will quickly find that they come in a wide variety of styles. The choice is yours, but there are a number of qualities or features that you will find particularly useful, and should look out for.

Chief among these is a removable bottom tray. As we'll learn, cages need to be cleaned out regularly, and this feature will make that task a lot easier.

Another important thing to look for is durable construction from tough wire. Guinea pigs love to gnaw, so make sure that yours won't be able to gnaw their way out. Wire is also a great choice for light and ventilation.

Whilst wire is best for walls, you want a solid metal or plastic floor. A wire mesh floor might sound convenient but is hard on soft feet, and can lead to bumblefoot (see later in this book).

Lastly, you should look out for hatches both on the top of the cage (so that you can reach in easily) and the side of the cage (so that your pet has a front door!).

The most important feature of your cavy cage will be the nest box where your pet will sleep. These are important because in the wild, a guinea pig will nest in a den or burrow, and the enclosed nest box emulates this cosy, enclosed environment.

Size-wise, a nest box only needs to be big enough to allow your guinea pig to turn around with 5-7.5cm of bedding in place. The entrance needs to allow for easy entry and exit, and at least one removable side is a must for easy cleaning. Wood is probably the best material for a nest box. Don't be tempted to just use cardboard—your cavy will chew its way through it in no time at all.

A final note: before you even start cage shopping, you should think about where the cage will reside in your home. The best places are zones where your cavy can see people coming and going, but at the same time isn't too disturbed by noise and motion. Anywhere near a noisy device such as a television, radio, or stereo is totally out, as is anywhere that is subject to a cold draught. Careful forethought is required!

Outdoor Housing

We've covered indoor housing above in some detail, but what if for some reason you need to keep your guinea pig(s) outdoors? It bears saying that it is better to keep guinea pig indoors, but if this is not possible, an excellent outdoor hutch will be essential—after all, it's the hutch that will keep your pets warm, dry and safe. Another possibility is that you might like to put your guinea pig outdoors in a play run during the day, and then bring them in at night. This is a nice idea that gives your cavy the best of both worlds—again, a good hutch will be important.)

Rabbit hutches and guinea pig hutches are generally identical, so it goes without saying that suitable hutches are abundantly available commercially from pet shops and the like. There are basically two types: those made of metal, and those made from wood and wire. Both are fine, though there are some key differences between the two. While they are very durable, easy to clean, and less expensive, metal hutches get hot in summer and cold in winter. Wooden hutches on the other hand are harder to clean, can be chewed, and can rot, but they look good and perform better in hot and cold weather.

Any good hutch will have a wire bottom so that droppings can fall through. You should cover at least a third of this though, as otherwise your cavy may get sore or even cut feet over time. Good weather proofing is also essential, and should include solid or canvas side panels to block out wind. Finally, the hutch must have a nest box, just as for an indoor cage.

So where should you position an outdoor hutch? The best locations are quiet, not exposed to extremes of temperature, well-ventilated, and safe from predators. Also, you want to position the hutch somewhere that is convenient for you, as your cavy will still need plenty of attention for you.

Some enthusiasts are against keeping guinea pigs outdoors, as they feel that the dangers from extreme temperatures, predators, and increased likelihood of neglect are too great. Having said that, other people keep their cavies outdoors and swear by it. It's fair to say that while keeping guinea pigs outside is certainly do-able, it does require more vigilance on your part to reduce the dangers.

Bedding

Like all of the pocket pets (a 'pocket pet' is any small mammal commonly kept as a pet, in case you didn't know!), guinea pigs need a soft removable material on the floor of their cages in order to be properly comfortable. The main function of this material is to be absorbent, so that the cage remains dry and odour-free between cleanings.

It used to be very common for cavies to have wood chips in their cages. However, some types of wood emit oils that can make cavies sick, and wood chips aren't very absorbent anyway. For these reasons they have fallen out of favour as a bedding material.

Most common these days is to use bedding made out of paper. This doesn't mean ripping up a few old newspapers! Many types of paper-based bedding for small pets are available commercially, and they are generally excellent. They differ in texture and appearance and in price, so experiment to find out which type suits you best. As a rule of thumb, lighter and softer paper beddings are more comfortable, and may be preferred by your pet, but are messier and mean a bit more work for you.

The idea with paper bedding is that you do spot replacements of soiled patches as needed, and do a thorough clean-out-and-replace weekly. That said, if you lay down a decently thick layer, you can actually get away with not replacing any bedding for a good four days at a stretch—it's just that good at capturing dampness and smells.

Also a good option, and one that is becoming more popular, is fleece bedding. This just means putting down a fleece blanket in the bottom of the cage, providing a soft, absorbent and easily washable floor layer. The benefits of this should be immediately obvious: it's cheaper to wash and reuse a blanket than it is to keep buying and throwing away paper bedding; it's quicker and easier to remove and insert a blanket than it is to replace a cage full of loose bedding; it looks very neat, and it's environmentally friendly.

Fleece bedding has its downsides though. It means doing a lot of extra laundry, and on top of that you need to use hot water and an unscented laundry detergent. It also means checking for and removing guinea pig poo on a daily basis—poo pellets are swallowed up by paper bedding, but with fleece they remain on top where they can be seen, trodden in, and so forth.

Feeding and Nutrition

Good nutrition is of course essential for maintaining cavy health and avoiding illness, just as it is for humans.

As mentioned previously, guinea pigs are highly adapted to eating grass and hay. You'll recall that guinea pigs practice coprophagy, which means that they eat their own soft faeces pellets in order to digest them again. This is perfectly normal and healthy for a guinea pig, so please try not to set aside your human sensibilities when you see it! So do you have to feed a pet cavy grass and/or hay? Yes! You should give your guinea pig constant access to grass or hay, so that they can spend enough time chewing to keep their teeth naturally ground down.

The following types of grass or grass hay are suitable: pasture hay; timothy hay; meadow hay; paddock hay; wheaten hay; oaten hay, ryegrass hay. However, Lucerne and clover hays are NOT suitable, as they contain too much protein and calcium.

Note that you can buy grass / grass hay from pet shops, but often it has sat a bit too long for optimum nutritional value, and is overpriced to boot. It's generally better to order it directly from a local farm, or through your exotics vet.

Other than grass and hay, your guinea pig's diet should mainly consist of fresh green vegetables and some quality commercial guinea pig pellets (for more on these, see below). On the vegetable side, these are all good choices: endive; broccoli; celery; cabbage; beetroot tops; carrot tops; Brussels sprouts; spinach; kale; dark leafed lettuce, and all Asian greens (bok choy and the like).

Guinea pig pellets

Guinea pig pellets are readily available at pet shops. They're specially formulated to contain everything that meets the nutritional requirements of guinea pigsand, in the right proportions.

When you're selecting pellets for your cavy, take the time to scan the nutritional information on the packet. A good protein level is about 16%, while fibre should always exceed 20%. Also, check the milling date, and try to avoid buying pellets that are more than 90 days old. Finally, for optimum freshness, store the pellets in an airtight container, and don't buy more pellets than your pet is likely to eat in a month.

The most important thing to remember with guinea pig pellets is not to overfeed with them. An adult guinea pig who is allowed to eat as many pellets as he or she likes will become obese—the same is not true of vegetables. (Note that overfeeding is not an issue for guinea pigs up to three months in age.)

As a rule of thumb, 1/8 of a cup of pellets per day is about right for a medium sized guinea pig, up to 1/4 of a cup for particularly big ones. You should split this ration into two and provide the feed at two meal-times each day, morning and night. Remove and discard any uneaten pellets after each meal.

Serving dish

Whatever you're serving up to your cavy, the question of what to serve it in is pretty simple. The best option is a heavy crock bowl—that is, a bowl made of earthenware. These are readily available to buy from pet shops, are easy to clean, are heavy enough not to get knocked over, and are un-chewable too.

Foods to avoid

The above menu—grass and grass hay, fresh leafy greens, commercial pellets—contains everything that your cavy needs, and you don't need to feed him or her anything else. But, the reality is that from time to time, you're going to be tempted to give your pet a little bit of some other food, perhaps something you're having for dinner. This might seem harmless, but it is not a good idea, and might make your cavy sick.

The following foods are not suitable for cavies, and should not be offered to them under any circumstances: cereals; grains; nuts, seeds; corn; beans; peas; breads; biscuits; sweets; sugar; breakfast cereals; chocolate; buttercups; garden shrubs; lily of the valley; onion grass; onions; potato tops; raw beans; beetroot; spinach and rhubarb leaves; pickled foods or any bulk plants (may cause digestive problems).

If you'd like to give your guinea pig a treat, carrots—rather than any of the above—are perfect. Also good are thin slices of fruit, such as apple, peach, orange or pear. You can buy commercially prepared guinea pig treats from a pet food shop, but they aren't really necessary if carrots or these fruits are available.

Water

Cavies should only ever be given water to drink, and should be provided with a constant, clean and fresh supply of it. It's tempting to just give it to them in a bowl, but the water in a bowl is likely to become soiled pretty quickly. The hygienic option is a bottle with a spring-loaded sipper spout. These are inexpensive and work well—just make sure that you get one with a stainless steel spout, as other materials will get chewed.

Grooming and Bathing

Guinea pigs are a dream to keep clean and well groomed. Their hair actually repels dirt, and like cats, they self-groom. This is enough to keep them clean in the ordinary course of events. However, that doesn't mean you shouldn't brush your cavy. Most guinea pigs enjoy being brushed and combed, and it's an opportunity for you to bond with your pet and to check for problems.

(The foregoing applies to short-haired cavies. If you have a long-haired cavy, you will need to brush it every day, as it won't be able to keep its coat free from mats by itself.)

Equipment-wise, you will need a brush and a comb in order to give your guinea pig the full salon experience. Go for a slicker or pin brush, as these types are gentle while still being effective. For a comb, a wide-toothed human comb is fine. Always brush first—in the direction the hair lies, not against it—starting with the head, then neck, back, front legs and hind legs, and lastly the belly. Avoid extra-sensitive areas such as around the eyes, and then once you're finished brushing, go back and do those areas with the comb.

You may find that a lot of hair falls out when you brush your cavy; this is normal, though the level varies throughout the year. Hair fall is at its peak in early autumn, as it makes way for fur that will keep your pet warm through the winter.

If you do need to bathe your guinea pig, just put a little lukewarm water at the bottom of a basin, and use a gentle shampoo, such as one for babies. Use a cup to wet your cavy's hair and to rinse off the shampoo, and dry by cuddling your pet in a towel. Try to avoid getting water in the eyes or ears.

Cleanliness

As you can see from the above, keeping a guinea pig clean and well-groomed is pretty much as easy as falling off a log. The same can't be said, unfortunately, of the cages they live in!

How and how often you clean your cavy's cage will depend on what type of bedding you are using. We mentioned above in the Bedding section that with paper bedding you can do spot replacements of soiled bedding as needed, and do a thorough clean-out-and-replace weekly. For paper bedding, this is a good plan.

For fleece bedding you will need to take it out, wash and replace the bedding around two times per week. Do not on any account simply drop a soiled fleece into the washing machine! Before it goes into the machine you will need to shake, vacuum, and vigorously brush the debris off of it. For the brushing, try a fingernail brush first, then a rubber mitt for the inevitable embedded hair.

No matter what kind of bedding you use, cleaning the cage itself follows the same routine. Here's how to do it:

1. First, remove your pet from its cage and place it somewhere safe while you work. A simple cardboard box will do, or give it someone else to hold while you clean.
2. Now remove everything from the cage, including water bottle, bowl, nest box and any toys. Take these to a sink so that you can clean them before returning them later.

3. Third, remove all bedding and loose material with a dustpan and brush. Use a fine brush to ensure that even small pieces of bedding etc., are removed.
4. Mix up a 50/50 solution of white vinegar and water in a spray bottle, and spray the cage all over with this solution. Wipe dry.
5. If necessary, apply some vinegar at full strength to any stubborn/problem areas. Rinse well.
6. Clean the water bottle, bowl etc. that you removed earlier.
7. Replace bedding, bowl, bottle etc…and you're done!

You might be wondering, why vinegar? Two reasons: first of all, vinegar is a powerful antibacterial agent. Also, it is an acid. Because urine is alkaline, the vinegar will cut right through urine and urine build-up.

Health and Illness

The normal lifespan for a guinea pig is about five to seven years, with an average of perhaps five-and-a-half years. The longest living guinea pig on record achieved the ripe old age of 15, but that sort of innings is of course highly unusual.

Of course you want your cavy to enjoy a long and healthy life, free from sickness as much as possible. There is good news here, as cavies are hardy, and when kept as pets, do not often fall ill. As already discussed, a good diet with fresh water and supplementary vitamin C goes a long way to keeping your guinea pig in rude good health (see above, 'Feeding and Nutrition'). However, they are susceptible to a few illnesses in particular, so you need to be mindful of these.

Like sailors and pirates on long sea voyages in the 15th century, cavies are prone to vitamin C deficiency (or scurvy). This is because like humans, but unlike most animals, guinea pigs are unable to synthesize their own vitamin C, and hence must get it through their diet.

Vitamin C deficiency primarily causes swollen joints, which will manifest itself as weakness, lethargy, and difficulty and pain while moving. Diarrhoea and a 'rough' coat are also symptoms.

Luckily, you don't have to feed your furry pal lemons to avoid vitamin C deficiency, because vitamin C is also present in the green and leafy vegetables that you were going to feed your cavy anyway.

Nevertheless, the occasional kiwi fruit (a very rich source of vitamin C) is a good idea. It is possible to give vitamin C as a supplement, added either to drinking water or to commercial feed, but it should really never be necessary.

Ulcerative pododermatitis, also known as bumblefoot, is another common cavy ailment. It is an infection and inflammation of the footpads, which cause them to become ulcerated and swollen. Common in birds and rodents of all types, it is caused in cavies by dirty wire or mesh flooring. The wire causes abrasions on the soft footpads, through which trace amounts of urine and faeces enter and cause infection. Bumblefoot is of course very painful. It's essential that you consult a vet if you think your guinea pig may have it. Your vet is likely to prescribe an antibiotic and possibly soaking the feet in a chlorhexidine solution.

Bumblefoot can be prevented through putting down a layer of cardboard or cloth on top of any mesh or wire flooring, and changing this soft layer regularly; a few times per week.

Dental problems are another potential difficulty for your pet, and the most common dental problem for cavies is called malocclusion. Malocclusion is where the front teeth don't align correctly, and it leads to them not wearing down normally and becoming overgrown. (Note that overgrown teeth can also occur when the diet contains too much soft food.) Malocclusion is genetic and must be treated by a vet.

Our last common health problem is mites, and specifically, the mite Trixacarus cavie. A guinea pig that is infested with this parasite will develop red and scabby bald patches on their coat. Mites must be treated by a vet. Don't delay seeing a vet, especially if you have more than one cavy, as mites spread very easily from one animal to another.

Finding a Vet

There's a fairly common misconception that the smaller the pet, the less need for a vet (excuse the pun!). In fact, cavies benefit greatly from a yearly check-up with a vet so that any problems are caught early. Also, should there be an emergency, you will want to have a familiar vet that you can consult immediately. A crisis situation is no time to be searching for a suitable medical professional.

So, for multiple reasons, it's important that you find a vet in your area and establish a relationship with him or her as soon as you get your cavy. Vets that treat guinea pigs (along with cats, dogs etc.) are known as 'small animal' vets. Not all vet clinics will treat guinea pigs, so call around to find one that does. Alternatively, you could ask your friends for a referral, or even consult an internet message board to get a recommendation from a fellow guinea pig fancier in your area.

Part 4: Guinea Pigs at Work and Play

The earlier parts of this book are all about the practicalities of guinea pigs and the keeping of them. History, diet, health, feeding, breeding and so on and so forth. All of that is important and necessary, but at the same time you should never forget that owning a pet is supposed above all to be FUN for you and for them, and that goes double for cavies! So, in this part, we focus on the good times you and your guinea pig(s) will have together.

Communication

One of your biggest responsibilities as a pet owner, after making sure your charge is clean, fed and sheltered, is to learn how to understand what your pet is communicating. Because you and your cavy don't share a spoken language, this communication will take place mostly via body language (though you can learn to understand your guinea pig's vocalisations too; see below).

'Popcorning' is just what it sounds like: jumping straight up in the air, usually multiple times. It's a sign of happiness and excitement. Licking you is, as for other pets, partly a way of getting the delicious salt off your skin! However, it is also a grooming behaviour and therefore a sign of trust—your cavy wouldn't lick someone he or she didn't trust.

Stretched-out cavies are feeling safe and relaxed, just like you when you might stretch out on a sofa or in hammock. Notice that stretching out leaves you pretty much defenceless, so it's something that you do only when you know that you are not in any danger—the same is true for guinea pigs.

Part 4:
Guinea Pigs at Work and Play

The earlier parts of this book are all about the practicalities of guinea pigs and the keeping of them. History, diet, health, feeding, breeding and so on and so forth. All of that is important and necessary, but at the same time you should never forget that owning a pet is supposed above all to be FUN for you and for them, and that goes double for cavies! So, in this part, we focus on the good times you and your guinea pig(s) will have together.

Communication

One of your biggest responsibilities as a pet owner, after making sure your charge is clean, fed and sheltered, is to learn how to understand what your pet is communicating. Because you and your cavy don't share a spoken language, this communication will take place mostly via body language (though you can learn to understand your guinea pig's vocalisations too; see below).

'Popcorning' is just what it sounds like: jumping straight up in the air, usually multiple times. It's a sign of happiness and excitement. Licking you is, as for other pets, partly a way of getting the delicious salt off your skin! However, it is also a grooming behaviour and therefore a sign of trust—your cavy wouldn't lick someone he or she didn't trust.

Stretched-out cavies are feeling safe and relaxed, just like you when you might stretch out on a sofa or in hammock. Notice that stretching out leaves you pretty much defenceless, so it's something that you do only when you know that you are not in any danger—the same is true for guinea pigs.

Sometimes you might go to pat your cavy on the head only for him or her to engage in head tossing, as if throwing your hand off. This behaviour means 'don't touch me', and it is a sign that you are touching (or attempting to touch) your pet in a way that he or she is not entirely comfortable with. Note that some guinea pigs are fine with being patted on the head, but others are simply not.

A stiffened body or legs is a defensive attitude, meant to ward off attacks, and is mostly reserved for other guinea pigs. It means 'back off'. If a guinea pig does this towards another guinea pig, and the other guy doesn't retreat, it's likely that a fight will ensue.

Bumping noses is a way of saying hello to another guinea pig, much like the Maoris of New Zealand performing a hongi.

You will hopefully never see your cavy playing dead, as it's the final defence tactic of a guinea pig that is feeling trapped and extremely frightened. The idea is to fool a predator into thinking that its prey is dead, and relaxing enough to give the cavy a chance to escape.

If your pet does this, it's almost certainly because of another animal; you should remove that animal immediately and pet your cavy to reassure it.

In addition to the body language listed above, cavies also communicate, in a limited way, through vocalisations. They coo at their young (and their owners, if they love them enough!), they squeal when they sense danger, and sometimes when they are begging for food, they gurgle when they are content, and they clack their teeth as a warning to back off. Pay attention to these noises, and together with your new knowledge of guinea pig body language, you won't miss a thing that your cavy is trying to tell you.

Training—Techniques

It is, of course, common to train your dog to obey your commands, and many dog owners do this. Less people train their cats, but is this because cats are untrainable, or is it just less important that your cat obey you?

The answer to this is somewhere in the middle. While it almost certainly IS less important to most people that their cat obey them, there are fundamental differences between cats and dogs that directly impact on their trainability. Dogs are by nature pack animals—descendants of animals that had to communicate and work together in order to bring down prey—while cats are solitary hunters without much reason to communicate or follow directions.

But what about guinea pigs? Well you will be delighted to find out that they are perfectly trainable. Not as biddable as dogs, but not as unco-operative as cats! Below, we'll look at some training techniques.

The first training technique we'll look at is called lure/reward training. It's pretty simple and it's used on lots of animals (including dogs). It goes like this:
1. Request—You make a request by giving a verbal command. 'Sit, Ubu, sit' or 'circle' or whatever it is that you would like your pet to do.
2. Lure—Here you show your pet a treat (more on the treat below) to entice him or her to comply with your request and perform the desired action.
3. Response—Your guinea pig performs the desired action! (You hope.)
4. Reward—In return for performing the action, you let your pet have the treat.

Pretty simple, right? It is. The trick, if you can call it that, is to use a treat that your cavy really loves. Their desire for the treat, plus consistency in your requests, will do the rest. Note that ideally you want to use a treat that you don't give your pet at other times. Using a treat that you also give your pet at other (non-training) times will only serve to confuse things. If you are stuck for an idea for a new healthy treat, here are some ideas: cantaloupe; blueberries; capsicum; carrots; parsley; lettuce. Don't forget to cut the treat food into really small pieces so that your cavy doesn't get full too quickly!

The other training technique that you might usefully employ is clicker training. Again, this technique is used on lots of animals, and in fact is a very popular method for training dogs. Like lure/reward training, clicker training uses treats. However, it also employs a device (the clicker), which is used to produce a stimulus (the click) that is linked to compliance with a command.

Ok, so first of all, what's a clicker? A clicker is a simply handheld device that makes a click-sound when pressed. They're widely available in pet stores and online and are fairly cheap. For a guinea pig, a clicker with a relatively quiet click is fine—a loud click can be a bit startling.

With clicker in hand, here's how it works: first you need your guinea pig to associate the click-sound with getting a treat. So you click the clicker, and give your guinea pig a treat. Then you do it again. And again.

Click-treat, click-treat, click-treat. Aim for about ten times in succession in total. Close timing is important: a click, and then immediately, a treat. Then start to leave a pause between clicks/treats, and vary the length of that pause. You might click-treat, wait three seconds, then click-treat, then eight seconds, then click-treat, then five seconds, click treat, and so on.

This first step is sometimes referred to as loading the clicker. Do it for a couple of sessions a day for 3-4 days and your cavy will expect a treat every time he or she hears a click. Once your clicker is loaded, you can proceed with the training proper.

Right. What you want to do now is to link the click-treat duo to the desired action or behaviour. There are a few different ways of causing the desired action to occur, and they are usually referred to as catching, shaping and luring.

Catching in this context just means that you watch your pet closely (clicker in hand, treat at the ready), wait for the desired action to occur by chance, and when it does: click-treat. Perhaps you want your guinea pig to run through a tunnel on command. So, you watch, wait for this to happen, and when it does, click-treat.

Catching behaviour has of course an obvious and massive flaw. What if your pet never performs the desired action? Ok, in that case you need to move on, and perhaps try shaping. Shaping in this context means building an action or behaviour by click-treating a series of small steps toward it. Using the above tunnel example, this would mean a click-treat when your guinea pig goes over to the tunnel, a click-treat for moving to the tunnel mouth, a click-treat for stepping inside, and so on.

Finally, we have luring. Luring involves using a treat and a hand gesture to induce the action. Going back to our tunnel example again, you would hold a treat in your hand and put it right in front of your cavy's nose. Then you would lead him or her by the nose, moving the treat towards the tunnel. As usual, when he or she completes the action—runs through the tunnel in this case—you click-treat. Luring can be the fastest way to get results, as it doesn't rely on the action happening by accident or by a series of small steps.

Whether you catch, shape or lure, there is a final step in clicker training, and it is adding the cue. The cue is the command word for the desired action, and it should only be added once the action/behaviour is 'shaped and strong'. Then what you want to do is simply to start saying the cue word aloud when you know the behaviour is about to occur. So the sequence becomes cue – action – reward (i.e. click-treat). After sufficient repetition, your cavy will learn what the cue means. At this point you can discontinue using the clicker for this action/behaviour though you will need to keep giving the reward!

Here are a few final tips and notes on training techniques:

- Don't attempt training sessions unless both you and your pet are in a good mood and are well rested;
- Once you've added a cue, don't reward if the action/behaviour occurs without the cue (this is known as 'stimulus control');
- Train in a quiet and calm environment at first, but add potential distractions over time for a higher degree of difficulty;
- Training is supposed to be fun, so if it is getting frustrating, take a break and come back to it later.

Training—Things to train

Alright, so you've read about lure/reward and clicker training, and they sound easy. But a guinea pig isn't a dog, so what are you going to train it to do exactly? Here are some suggestions.

Hopping through a hoop is a perennial favourite. The goal here is that your guinea pig will eventually leap through a hoop raised about 2.5 cm off the ground, on command. Not a bad trick, and relatively easy to train. You can easily use a shaping technique here, where you reward first of all just walking close to the hoop, then coming a bit closer, then walking through it, and so on.

Touching a ball at the end of a stick is a really useful thing to train your guinea pig to do. The ball and stick could just be a sponge ball on the end of a pencil, or there are commercial target sticks available, some with clickers built into the handle.

Again, this trick can again be taught effectively through shaping. First reward just looking at the stick, then moving towards it, and then touching it (with a nose, not a paw, if that wasn't already obvious!). Vary distance from the stick and height and position of the stick once you've got the basics in the groove.

The great thing about this trick is that once your cavy is reliably touching the ball, you can start to make it a moving target, so that you can walk your pet anywhere you like just by moving a stick. Very useful for getting it to come out from under the couch and return to its cage! Standing up and begging is a neat trick for guinea pigs just as it is for dogs, and it's easy to train using lure/reward or clicker training with luring. Start by holding a treat and letting your pet smell it and bump it with their nose. Then start to raise the treat. If your cavy follows at all, give then a reward (which could be a piece of the treat). Then rinse and repeat, getting higher and higher each time. Once the standing and begging is shaped and strong, add a cue word (we suggest 'stand'!).

If you'd like to get more ideas for tricks to teach your cavy, a quick internet search will turn up plenty of good suggestions.

Toys

Readers with children will know how important toys are. They will also know that no matter how expensive or lavish the toy, the cardboard box that it came in is almost always more interesting! The situation is not dissimilar with guinea pigs. Read on for toy ideas that will keep your cavies busy and happy. First on our list are chew toys. Guinea pigs love to chew, and it helps to keep their teeth healthy, so chew toys are kind of a must-have. You might be thinking that chew toys would be made out of some type of rubber, but actually the best chew toys are those made from willow. Try a willow tunnel, a willow ball or even just a set of willow chew sticks. Cavies love to munch on them and they're totally safe too. They won't last forever of course, but they aren't meant to and they're cheap anyway.

Next are the floor toys. These are the toys that you put out when you let your pets out for 'floor time' outside of their cages. You want to encourage your guinea pigs to run around and get some exercise, so this class of toys includes all balls. You can get ping pong balls, balls that contain a bell and rattle when rolled around, or the other option is to invest in some 'treat' balls. Treat balls can be opened up so that you can put some chopped herbs or vegetables inside. They have small holes all over them, so cavies love to push them around and nibble at the contents through the various holes. These are a real winner.

Now for the miscellaneous category:

- For whatever reason, many cavies really like pine cones, and as these are chewable and cheap to obtain, there's really no reason not to get some for your pet.
- Or you could try an old sock filled with hay—fun to push around and try to get into.
- Finally for the miscellaneous category, there's the good old toilet roll tube. Anything cardboard will have a very short life if given to a guinea pig of course, but toilet roll tubes are free and fun while they last.

Environment

if you have a baby who is learning to walk, it's best to 'toddler-proof' your home. So too it is with guinea pigs! While your guinea pig will probably spend most of his or her time in a cage, you will want to take it out often for playtime, to explore and so on. So, before taking a cavy into your home, you definitely want to do a sweep to make sure that it is going to be a safe environment and one that your pet won't easily be able to destroy.

Probably the biggest worry with guinea pigs when they are out and about is their propensity to gnaw things. Their sharp little incisors will make short work of wood and plastic, and this makes power cables a primary area of concern. The soft plastic cladding on an ordinary power cable provides very little protection for the wires within, and if your guinea pig chews through the cladding on a (live) power cable, electrocution and potentially even a fire can result.

Clearly then you want to give your guinea pig absolutely no opportunity ever to snack on a power cable. The best solution is to take all your power cables up off ground level, so that they are well out of reach for a ground-based rodent. If this isn't possible, the next best thing is to clad your low-lying power cables with something that will defeat little teeth—a harder plastic sheath, such as aquarium or electrical tubing, is readily available and ideal for this task.

After power cables, the next thing to consider is wooden furniture. Not all guinea pigs like to chew on wooden furniture, but many do. This is not dangerous for your pet, but it is of course dangerous to the aesthetics of your furniture! What to do about this? It is a difficult problem, as we're most likely talking about multiple large items of furniture such couches, tables, chairs and even doors.

There are two main solutions to the chewing-on-furniture problem. The first is to coat the items that your rodent wants to chew on (unfortunately you might need to learn which items these are by trial and error!) with something that is non-toxic but nasty-tasting or smelling to a guinea pig. Lemon juice is an obvious choice, or you could try perfume or cologne. Or, there are somecommercially available options. Test the lemon juice on a normally out-of-sight area of the piece of furniture first, just to make sure that it won't stain.

The other solution is to give your cavy something else to chew on that he or she will prefer. This is a pretty effective tactic if you choose the right chewable toy—your cavy will simply lose interest in the furniture if presented with something better. As we noted above, one of the best options here is a tunnel or ball or other toy made out of woven willow twigs. Cavies love to chew on these and they're 100% safe.

Cats and dogs are another thing to think about, environment-wise. Remember that in the wild, cats and dogs are descended frompredators, while guinea pigs are very firmly in the 'prey' category. This means that a guinea pig can arouse predatory instincts in even the most placid, well-fed, or lazy of cats/dogs. Having said that, most cats and dogs are fine with cavies, most of the time. They will accept a guinea pig into the home, be curious, even want to play with their new housemate. DON'T BE FOOLED into thinking this behaviour means that your cat or dog will never attack your cavy! No matter how harmonious things seem, you MUST keep in mind that nothing will ever change the predator/prey relationship, and NEVER leave a guinea pig alone with a dog or cat.

Next on our list is hidey holes, and by this we mean any hole or gap or space big enough for a cavy to squeeze into, and small enough, or positioned in such a way, that getting him or her out would be difficult or impossible or at the least awkward or annoying! Cavies love to get into spaces like this of course, but as a pet owner, it's a problem when you want to leave the house but you can't get your guinea pig out from under the couch to put him back in his cage!

The answer here is fairly obvious: plug all the gaps! There isn't a nook, crevice or crack that can't be blocked off with some creative thinking and a few basic materials. Poisonous plants are the final fly in the ointment of a safe and secure home environment for your furry little friend. You COULD learn exactly which plants are and aren't safe for your pet to take a bite out of, but please don't: it is far easier and safer to simply take all potted plants in your home up and out of reach.

Once you've attended to all of the above, do a final sweep of your home to make sure that: 1) there's nothing chewable (shoes, magazines, mobile phones…) on the floor; there are no cords dangling to floor level, and that cupboards can't be accessed or opened. Job done!

Adding Playmates

Getting one guinea pig is a bit like having your first child. At first, one seems like enough, but pretty soon you start thinking that maybe he or she would really like to have a little playmate. Guinea pigs are social animals and they do get lonely, so if you can possibly accommodate a second, you should definitely go for it.

(Earlier in this book we discussed the practical considerations of having more than one guinea pig. There's no need to repeat that information here, except to mention that you do need of course to think about these practical consideration before taking the plunge on a playmate for your pet.)

The great thing about having more than one cavy is that you can watch them live and play together without having to get involved yourself. Their little interactions are fun, interesting, and frankly just a joy to behold, and will give you a lot of pleasure—make no mistake about that.

One quite amusing example of different behaviour when you have multiple cavies instead of just one is there competition for food. Single guinea pigs can be quite fussy eaters, but as soon as there is someone else around 'competing' for the same food, they almost always find that they are fine with eating whatever you serve up.

In short, two or more guinea pigs will play together, chase each other, snuggle together, and generally just keep each other healthy and happy!

Conclusion

We started out this book by noting that guinea pigs have been a popular pet since at least the late 16th century. Has reading it convinced you to join the ranks of the many, many guinea pig owners and aficionados around the world? We hope so!

As you can tell, guinea pigs offer a very different pet-owning experience from the run-of-the-mill cat or dog, and they really inspire passion in their owners. It's true that there is more work than you might think in having a healthy and happy guinea pig, but it's really not too bad, and the rewards make the work more than worth it.

If you would like to know more, there are of course any number of books, articles, videos and forums online that can answer any other questions that you might have. Good luck!

Naming Your Pet

Why do we name our pets? The pets themselves don't seem to care one way or the other, so I guess at the end of the day, we do it for ourselves. But whatever the reason, for the vast majority of people, naming pets is a mandatory (not to mention fun) part of having them.

Naming a guinea pig isn't the same as naming a dog, cat, or horse, of course. Guinea pigs have their own particular look and their own particular set of idiosyncrasies. Rex, Rufus, Flash, Arabian Knight, Tiddles, Mr Meowgi—these names just don't suit nervy, twitchy, cute, pint-sized rodents!

So what works? Funny names, silly names and cute names seem to fit best. Food-based names are also good. Still stuck? Don't worry! Because below are 201 of the very best cavy names, hand-picked just for you. (If you can't decide go for Lambchop or Meatball)

1. Ant
2. April
3. Archie
4. August
5. Autumn
6. Bailey
7. Bam
8. Banana
9. Bart
10. Basil
11. Bean
12. Beauty
13. Bella
14. Benny
15. Bingo
16. Biscuit
17. Blob
18. Blueberry
19. Bond
20. Boris
21. Bracken
22. Bradley
23. Bramble
24. Brandy
25. Broccoli
26. Brownie
27. Bubbles
28. Buddy
29. Bug
30. Butter
31. Caesar
32. Candy
33. Caramel
34. Charlotte
35. Chelsea
36. Chesney
37. Chewbacca
38. Chilli
39. Chloe
40. Chocolate
41. Chris
42. Chunky
43. Cinnamon
44. Cola
45. Cookie
46. Corrie
47. Cotton
48. Crackers
49. Cream
50. Crumpet
51. Destiny
52. Dixie
53. Dizzy
54. Dolly
55. Domino
56. Dotty
57. Doughnut
58. Dudley
59. Dumpling
60. Eve
61. Ezra
62. Fern
63. Flash
64. Flower
65. Fluffy
66. Forest
67. Frisky
68. Fudge
69. Fuzz
70. Gadget
71. Ginger
72. Gingerbread
73. Gizmo
74. Goldie
75. Grape
76. Gremlin
77. Hannah
78. Harley
79. Harriet
80. Hansel
81. Heather
82. Honey
83. Hope
84. Hopper
85. Iceman
86. Isabell
87. Izzy
88. Jake
89. Jamie
90. January
91. Jasper
92. Jedi
93. Jelly
94. June
95. Kosmo
96. Kramer
97. Lambchop
98. Larry
99. Laser
100. Layla
101. Lenny
102. Liam
103. Lily
104. Llama
105. Loo
106. Lucky
107. Lucy
108. Mandy
109. Marbles
110. March
111. Maize
112. Marmalade
113. Marshmallow
114. Marvin
115. May
116. Meatball
117. Midnight
118. Milly
119. Milo
120. Mistletoe
121. Misty
122. Mocha
123. Monday
124. Monty
125. Mothball
126. Motley
127. Mr Poops
128. Muffin
129. Mumbles
130. Murphy
131. Mystic
132. Nibbles
133. November
134. Nutmeg
135. Oreo
136. Ozzy
137. Pancake
138. Panda
139. Patch
140. Peanut
141. Peaches
142. Pebbles
143. Pepper
144. Pepsi
145. Piglet
146. Pip
147. Pippin
148. Pixie
149. Polly
150. Poppy
151. Pudding
152. Pumpkin
153. Rainbow
154. Raisin
155. Rascal
156. Rocky
157. Ruby
158. Russell
159. Salty
160. Sam

161. Sammy
162. Sarah
163. Scooter
164. Scout
165. Shaggy
166. Skittle
167. Slash
168. Sleepy
169. Smokey
170. Smudge
171. Sneezy
172. Snickers
173. Snoopy
174. Snowy
175. Snuffle
176. Snuggles
177. Sonic
178. Sooty
179. Sparkle
180. Speckles
181. Spike
182. Squeaks
183. Star
184. Strawberry
185. Stripes
186. Summer
187. Sunshine
188. Tango
189. Teddy
190. Thumper
191. Tic
192. Timmy
193. Toffee
194. Trixie
195. Truffles
196. Twix
197. Wednesday
198. Whiskey
199. Wombat
200. Yellow
201. Zips

CPSIA information can be obtained at www.ICGtesting.com
Printed in the USA
LVIW01n1440210316
480091LV00030B/863